The Waterman/Harewood Piano Series

Piano Playtime Book One

*Very first solos and duets
written, selected and edited by*

Fanny Waterman

and

Marion Harewood

Faber Music Limited

London

Contents

Nos. 1–7: separate hands
Nos. 8–16: alternating hands
Nos. 18–21, 27 and 28: both hands in similar motion
Nos. 22–26 and 29: both hands independent

© 1978 by Faber Music Ltd
First published in 1978 by Faber Music Ltd
3 Queen Square, London WC1N 3AU
Music drawn by Michael Terry
Illustrations by Anne Shingleton
Cover design by Shirley Tucker
Printed in England by Belmont Press Ltd
All rights reserved

1 Marching

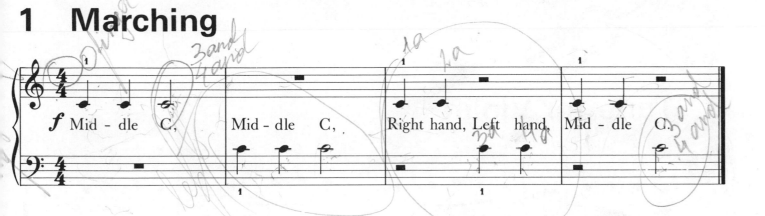

Mid – dle C, Mid – dle C, Right hand, Left hand, Mid – dle C.

2 Swinging

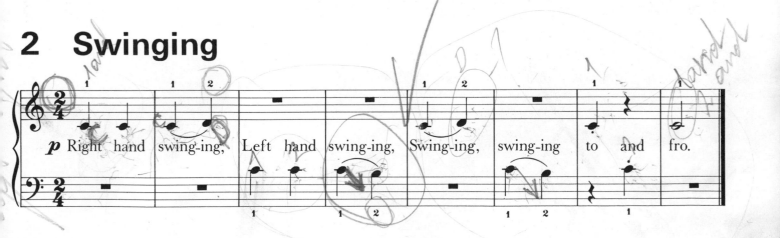

Right hand swing-ing, Left hand swing-ing, Swing-ing, swing-ing to and fro.

3 Look at me, E F G

Look at me, E F G, Down to E and back to C.

4 Hear me play, C B A

mf Hear me play C B A, Down to G and back to C.

5 Tune for Violin

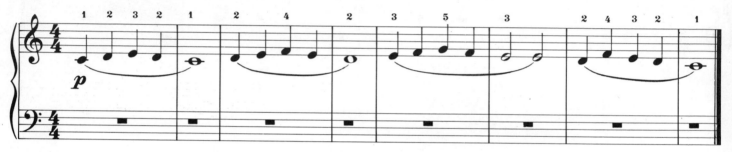

6 Tune for Cello

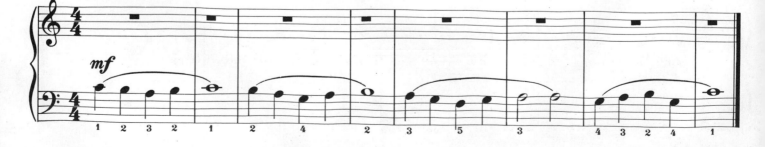

7 Waltz (Duet)

Ferdinand BEYER
(1805–1863)

8 Yankee Doodle

Traditional American

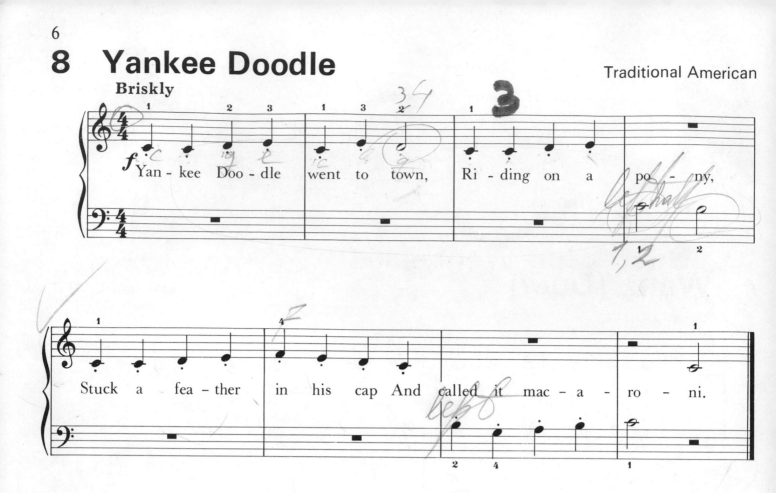

Yan - kee Doo - dle went to town, Ri - ding on a po - ny,

Stuck a fea - ther in his cap And called it mac - a - ro - ni.

9 On the Bridge at Avignon

Traditional French

Sur le pont d'A - vi - gnon, L'on y dan - se, l'on y dan - se,

Sur le pont d'A - vi - gnon, L'on y dan - se tout en rond.

10 Good King Wenceslas

Traditional Carol

Maestoso

f Good King Wen - ces - las looked out | On the feast of | Ste - phen,

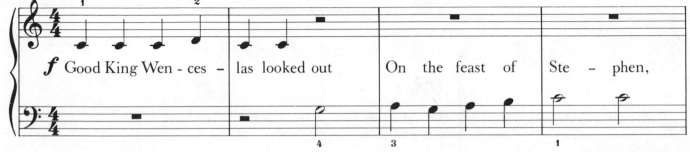

When the snow lay round a – bout, Deep and crisp and e – ven.

Bright - ly shone the moon that night, Though the frost was cru - el,
mf

When a poor man came in sight, Gath'- ring win - ter fu - - el.
f

11 Bugle Call

F. W.

12 Frère Jacques

Traditional French

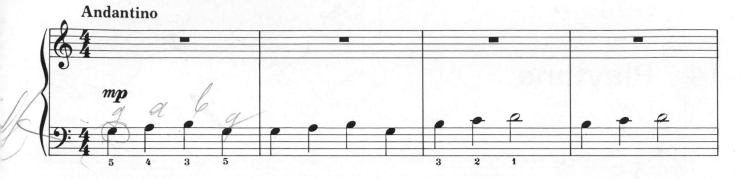

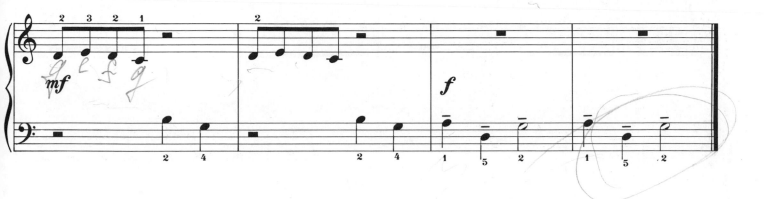

13 Russian Song

Arr. M. H.

14 Playtime

F. W.

Allegro moderato

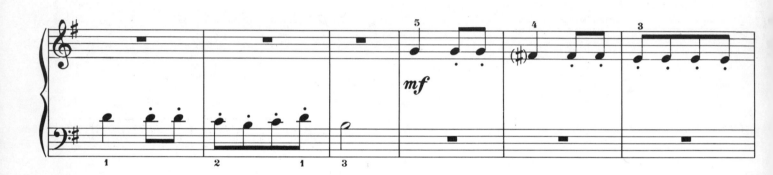

15 Clapping Song

Engelbert HUMPERDINCK (1854–1921) Arr. M. H.

With my hands I clap, clap, clap
With my feet I tap, tap, tap
Left foot first, right foot then,
Round about and back again.

Scherzando

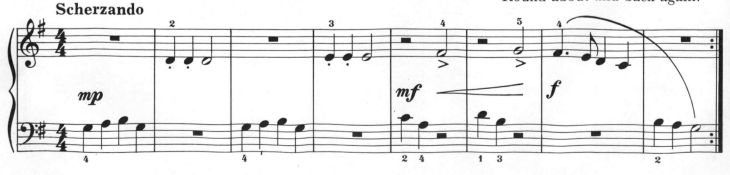

16   Fairy Waltz 5

F.W.

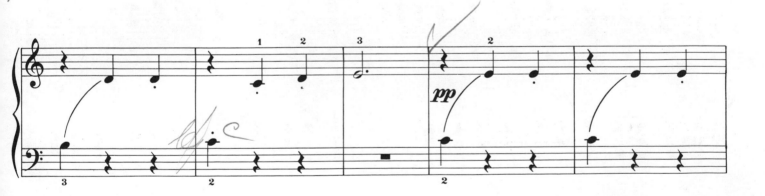

17 Theme and Six Variations

Ferdinand BEYER

Moderato   Secondo

17 Theme and Six Variations

Ferdinand BEYER

Primo

18 Hungarian Song

F. W.

19 The Roundabout

Louis KOHLER
(1820–1886)

20 Chatterbox

Carl CZERNY
(1791–1857)

Con moto

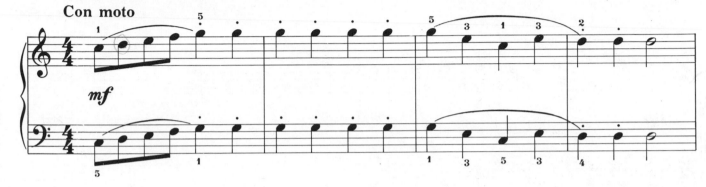

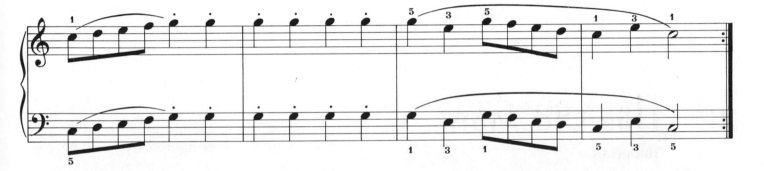

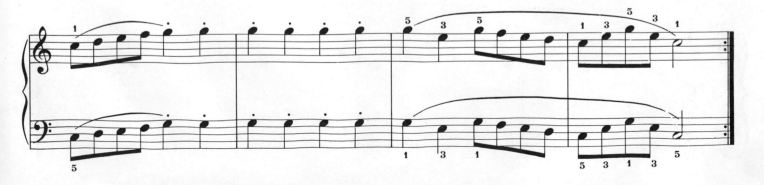

21 Lullaby

Traditional German

22 This Old Man

Children's Folk Song
collected by Cecil Sharp

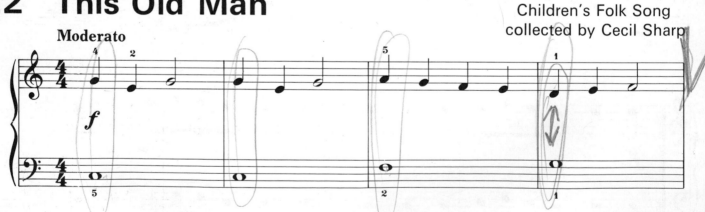

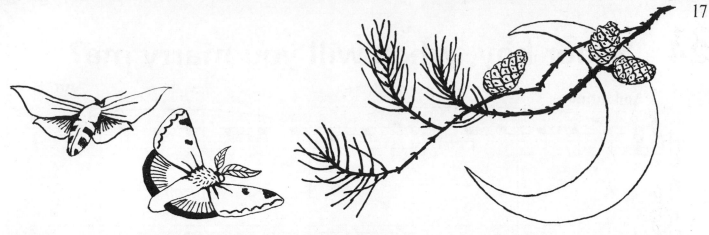

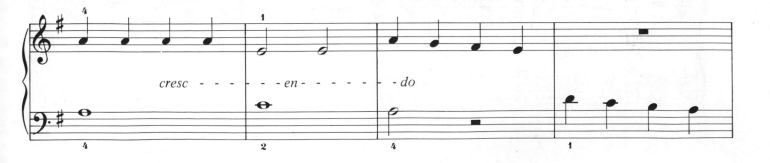

24 Sailor boy, when will you marry me?

Arr. F. W.

25 Cuckoo, here comes the Spring

Traditional German

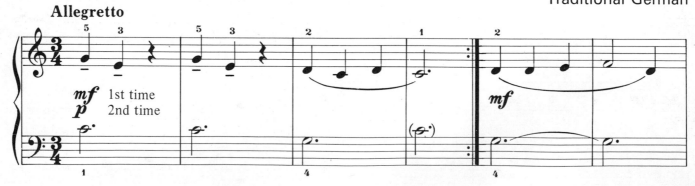

26 Oranges and Lemons

Traditional English

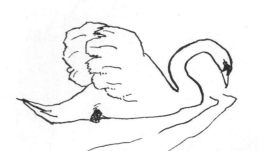

27 On the Lake

Ferdinand BEYER

Secondo

27 On the Lake

Ferdinand BEYER

Primo

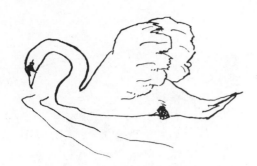

28 Mother's Day

Josef GRUBER

Secondo

28 Mother's Day

Josef GRUBER

Primo

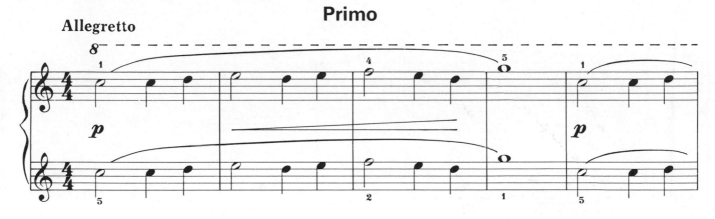

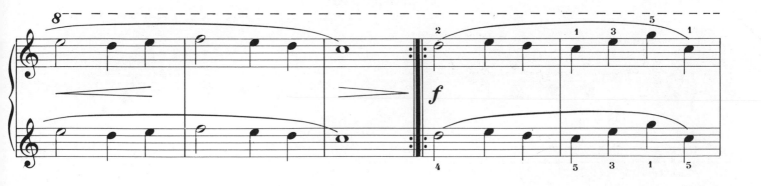

29 Cradle Song

Russian Lullaby

Primo

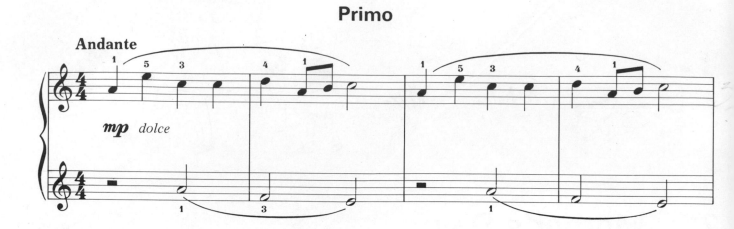

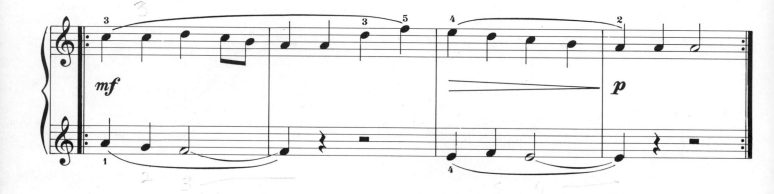

Secondo